MA

WORLDS

Derrick Wallace

Manz Dem

europe books

© 2022 Europe Books| London
www.europebooks.co.uk | info@europebooks.co.uk

ISBN 979-12-201-2106-4
First edition: May 2022
Distribution for the United Kingdom: **Vine House Distribution ltd**

Printed for Italy by Rotomail Italia S.p.A. – Vignate (MI)
Stampato presso Rotomail Italia S.p.A. - Vignate (MI)

Manz Dem

Acknowledgements

First and foremost, I would like to thank the God of Abraham for strength and guidance regarding this project.

My beautiful wife Mercy Lynn for her warm smile and encouragement.

Simon (Cassidy Guitars) for artist endorsement.

Andy (Dovetail Strings).

Dr Simon Fraser-Clark (Laney Amplification).

All staff (Europe Books).

Cousin Andrea Smikle (for believing).

Last but no means least the ManZ Dem.

Dedicated to

Cleveland Wallace (16.06.57 – 02.08.20)
1st Teacher. Loving Brother.
Never Forgotten!

Table of Contents

Manz Dem Track Listing/ Artists

1. **Konig:** *You're The One*
2. **Ciyo Brown:** *Similitude*
3. **Reuben Reynolds:** *Anticipate*
4. **Chris Cobson:** *Bele*
5. **Ivan Christie:** *Calm Waters*
6. **Paul Williams:** *He Makes Me Smile*
7. **Tony Remy:** *Lighthouse*
8. **Cameron Pierre:** *Big Foot*
9. **Edison Herbert:** *Why Not*
10. **Ollie Pinnock:** *Smile*
11. **Andrew Smith:** *Pushing*
12. **Dee Ral:** *Still In Love With You*
13. **Joseph Ross:** *You Know Our Day Will Come*
14. **Ian Lewinson:** *Pushback*
15. **Tony Bean:** *Heaven*

Foreword
Manz Dem:

15 hunks of delectable silky smooth chocolate coated skin, wrapped in a variety of flags capable of playing the heck out of one of the world's most versatile instruments; the guitar. Some are single (Ladies!!) Others are taken (Argh!!). All in all, they have made some of the most important contributions to the British Music Industry for the past three decades and counting.

Let me say this from the off it is a collaborative effort!

Without the consent and enthusiasm of the artists involved, this project couldn't be conceived, never mind getting off the ground. *Manz Dem* is not about having a gripe or pointing the finger of blame at British Society; no rather we are all about celebrating each other's achievements, musicality, diversity, success and in the process formulating a new community of brotherhood and hopefully masculinity and empowerment.

Why now?

There is an old Jamaican saying:

"Do sumting before sumting do yuh"

Simply meaning seize the moment, don't sit around waiting for things to happen create something in case; unseen events befall you. No time in the history of present mankind is this sage advice relevant. With the pandemic sweeping nations, it is a painful reminder that we are extremely fragile and that tomorrow isn't promised. I therefore decided that this needed sorting before '***We all popped our clogs'***.

As with any good project, there needs to be a framework of contextualisation and in this case an important, cultural, social and historic one at best to inform you the consumer of the backdrop from whence this work commenced.

In 2007 I was extremely honoured to have written the first book (***50 Guitarists***) ever dedicated to British Guitarists who were based and performing in the British Isles. What set the book apart was that it covered new ground. My primary concern was for practitioners of the instrument we all know and love who were being eluded of exposure to a wider demographic of music lovers.

50 Guitarists is still spoken of today and there are calls for an urgent reprint of the text! However, instead, I have chosen to utilise the methodology of the book in a more streamlined fashion. The premise this time around focuses on 2 main themes:

1. *All Guitarists featured are male (gender)*
2. *Demographic: African/Caribbean/Duel Heritage/ (ethnicity)*

There are more startling gaps that need to be filled with the utmost urgency which the Manz Dem project seeks to address!

Q: Where may I purchase a work/text which highlights: The achievements of the UK Black Community of Guitarists?

Q: Why has it taken so long?

I don't want to spoil the film by giving away the plot of the story! Again, we have to look at the climate and conditions which these artists were trying to make headway. The 80s 90s and 00s was a fascinating time in the UK. Urban was all the rage albeit with a white face! It was not an uncommon sight to see more black session guitarists than ones who were signed in their own right.

Man Ah fih eat fuud.

One or two, perhaps three did make it. But the level of career support, investment and marketing was paucity to say the least. Exposure on daytime television or any television was rare. If one did make an appearance, again it is in the capacity of being a hired hand, behind the scenes so to speak. In short: a travesty.

Compare this in contrast:

"And now ladies and gentlemen, let's welcome Downbeat Recipient Artist of The Year for Guitar (1976) the one and only Mr. George Benson" (Applause)

"Hello, may I speak to Mrs. Foster?" "Yes, Mrs. Foster here how may I help you?" Yes, it's about your son Ronny. I just love the way he plays the keyboards may I have your permission to take him out on the road with me? "Excuse me; who am I talking too?" (Mrs. Foster) "Oh! I'm sorry my name's George Benson. I've just won" "I know who you are Mr. Benson" (Mrs. Foster) "You do realize Ronny is only 16? Please, come back when he finishes his schooling and then you will have our blessing to take him on the road".

There have been markedly improvements and kudos to shows which attempted to broaden the spectrum of music to UK audiences. Bob Marley the young dreadlock forming guitarist from Jamaica on **The Old Grey Whistle Test (1973), Top of the Pops (1970s), The Tube (1980s), Jools Holland (1990s), Jazz 606 (1990s)**.

However, the tremendous opportunities of connecting with new audiences globally via social media and streaming the possibilities are endless. It is imperative to buck the trend of miniscule documentation for black guitarists operating from the UK.

This project goes some way to redress the imbalance. I have derived great pleasure in how the project has taken on a life of its own. Initially, my mind was fixated on the idea of guitarists who I knew personally. Notwithstanding, the artists themselves mentioned, "Do you know such and such" or "This man says you fih hail him" because they like the sound of the project.

If I may indulge, it is a bold attempt to document a portion of the fantastic guitarists whilst they are still alive. There were many more that could have and ought to have been included yet I feel more than happy with the immediate selection who represent stylistic excellence and variety.

In closing I salute the "Manz Dem" for helping to cement their own legacy as well as contributing to the legacy of others. The biggest achievement we all could ask from this venture is that it will be a source of inspiration and reference for successive generations of guitarists from the UK Black Community long after we have departed.

Let them take the baton and run to the higher heights of artistic and creative expression, birthed in universal brilliance. Amen

"Time waiteth for no man"

Derrick Wallace

Konig

Konig

Konig - German word for "king" - was born Derrick Wallace in the leafy suburb of Edgbaston Birmingham of Jamaican parents whose roots are actually Ghanaian (Father) and South African (Mother).

Even though he was born in the United Kingdom, he perceives himself as an offshore African! Konig's career kicked off at age 15 when he attended Birmingham Guitar School and later studied jazz guitar at Goldsmiths, University in London at 17.
He then attended the Royal Birmingham Conservatoire following which he taught music around the United Kingdom. Whilst still a student, he was recruited by the international legend Jamaican jazz saxophonist, Andy Hamilton to join his band the Blue Notes.

The band performed on radio, television and a British tour to promote the *Jamaica by Night* album. Konig eventually left the Blue Notes to study jazz at the Julia Crane School of Music in New York where he fell under the mentorship of Yamaha endorsee and world-renowned big band conductor/composer Prof Bret Zvacek.

He was signed by Revolver Music in the early 2000 and his first album New Leaf debuted at number 8 on the UK based Radio WM album charts. During this period, Konig was chosen by Westone, a guitar manufacturing company to endorse and demonstrate their new Westone Corsair Classic guitar range.

The ultra-talented guitarist has played with various musicians from different genres of music but treasures most his opportunity of playing with Grammy winning Reggae Artist Michael Rose (Black Uhuru).

Besides the UK he has performed in many other countries namely Europe, Ireland, Canada, USA, Jamaica, and South Africa.

Konig is also the author of *50 Guitarists*:

"The first book of its kind to feature UK based guitarists that are often hidden from the mainstream by the music mafia".

Frederick Thelonious Baker
Artiste in Residence Royal Birmingham Conservatoire

1. Questions to answer (**Konig Answers/Response)**

- **Influences:** Whatever takes my interest at that particular moment; I'm very eclectic.
- **Inspirations:** In life my main influence is **Marcus 'Mosiah' Garvey** but my musical influence especially in my 20s was **Phil Keaggy**.
- **Albums: Captain's Journey** (*Lee Ritenour*) **Electric Guitarist** (*John Mclaughlin*) **Mint Jams** (*Casiopea*) **In Flight** (*George Benson*) **Opening Night** (*Kevin Eubanks*) **Town to Town** (*Phil Keaggy*) **Revelation** (*Phil Upchurch*) **Paz Are Back** (*Paz*).
- **Styles guitarists:** Right now, I've gone back to the '**South African School of Guitar**'.

My 1st professional teacher was the late great South African guitarist Russell Herman who taught me the importance of 'sound' and how to use the many inversions to great effect! Jonathan Butler, Keenan Ahrends, Vuma Levin, Johnny Fourie, Reza Khota, Bruce Muirhead, Alvin Dyers, Captain 'Mac' Mckenzie, Dylan Fine, Issy Ariefdien, Jonathan Crossley and Michael Bester are the guitarists from South Africa whom I enjoy listening to right now. They are extremely versatile and play in a myriad of styles, World Music, Jazz Rock, Classical, Fusion, Big Band and Goema.

An insight into the person behind the music section

- **What set you on the path of music in the 1st place?**

My sister in law's brother placed a guitar in my hands aged 15. Taking me to the Birmingham Guitar School and sowing the 'academic' seed set me on the path for music.

- **Where did you grow up; was it a musical environment?**

I grew up in Smethwick (Sandwell). My immediate environment wasn't that musical. However, the city of Birmingham's musicians from the African Caribbean community were very musical; looking back they created an exceptional musical environment to learn and grow.

- **What academic subjects did you study growing up did you plan on being a musician?**

I was extremely fond of Maths; those old books with the tables for Trigonometry, Art and Human Biology. Somewhere however I lost focus with my secondary schooling and didn't quite fulfil my potential! My intention was not to be a musician growing up.

- **1st Guitar? How did you acquire it?**

Gibson Les Paul Custom Copy (Cherry Sunburst Satellite) A friend of one of my sisters gave me £10 towards the guitar. I saved the other £40 and was able to obtain my 1st instrument for £50!

- **If you had a choice of any guitar in the world?**

(a) What would it be?

Soderlund Guitars (South African company) Loerie Model

(b) Would you play it or put it on the wall?

I'd buy two! One for playing/ recording; and the other would be on the wall as an artwork to admire the aesthetic beauty of the instrument

(c) Any other response? No!

(d) Why did you choose this track?

Musical dexterity, an example of group interplay

(e) How would you like to be remembered?

A man of vision, seeing what is possible before it is done, rather than after.

(f) Closing remark(s)

Enjoy Life!

Dr Ernest Ranglin O.D (Jamaica)

Soderlund Guitar Instrument of desire Konig

Ciyo Brown

Born in Jamaica, **Ciyo** arrived in England at the age of six months old. Though a high academic achiever qualifying as a Fellow of the Chartered Institute of Legal Executives and specializing in the area of Housing Law, music has always been a dedicated and professionally nurtured constant in Ciyo's journey through life. Ciyo is also a University Lecturer.

From early beginnings having first been taught to play the guitar at the age of nine by his father Lorenzo Alexander Brown, Ciyo has participated musically in theatre, studio recordings and live performances alongside a parade of internationally acclaimed artists. These have included Meli'sa Morgan, Glen Jones, Melba Moore, Shirley Jones, Jean Carne, China Moses, YolanDa Brown, Suggs, Caron Wheeler, Soul II Soul, Jazz vocal sensation Vimala Rowe, Ann Nesby (Sounds of Blackness), Ruby Turner, Royal Wedding vocalist Paul Lee, Annie Lennox, Jason Rebello, Soca Queen Alison Hinds, Jazz Warriors, Tomorrow's Warriors, Talvin Singh, LCGC, East London Gospel Choir, Chevelle Franklin, Andy Hamilton, Chakademus and Pliers, The I-Threes (Marcia Griffith, Judy Mowatt and Marcia Griffiths, Reggae Philharmonic Orchestra, Urban Soul Orchestra, Alex Wilson, Sonny Okusons, internationally acclaimed jazz guitarists Martin Taylor, Giorgio Serci, Nigel Price, Jim Mullen, Dave Cliff, Femi Temowo, legendary James Brown saxophonist Pee Wee Ellis, Sly and Robbie, Freddie McGregor, Little Roy, Adele Harley, Steel Pulse and Carleen Anderson. Ciyo has also been appointed as Musical Director for a range or coveted artists to include the likes of Ronnie Laws, Billy Paul, Hil St Soul, Horace Andy, Johnny Clarke, Greg Kofi-Brown (of Osibisa fame) and Ann Nesby (of Sounds of Blackness fame).

An in-demand musicians' musician, Ciyo's ongoing collaborative works cover a range of genres. His talent has enhanced iconic popular music alongside artists such as Roachford, Raghav, Shara Nelson, through progressive Jazz with Soweto Kinch, to the 'new psychedelia' Brit-pop/folk influenced music of Bishi. Ciyo's Jazz guitar contributions are also present in the genres of reggae and lover's rock and can be found in his live and recorded work with many artists including John Holt, Carroll Thompson, Janet Kay, JC Lodge, Ken Boothe, Sugar Minott, Bob Andy, Legendary Jamaican guitarist Earl 'Chinna Smith', Barry Biggs, Dennis Bovell, Pam Hall, Jimmy Lindsay, Earl 16, Lukie D, Paulette Tajah, Susan Cadogan, Lorna Bennett, Kofi, Winston Reedy, Christopher Ellis and internationally acclaimed vocalist Luciano.

Ciyo has toured with Courtney Pine, Byron Wallen, Ronnie Laws, Billy Paul, Jean Toussaint, Maxi Priest, Beres Hammond, Horace Andy, Cleveland Watkiss, Steel Pulse, Linda Lewis, Alex Webb's Café Society Swing All Stars and a host of others to include Royalty in Lady Gabriella Windsor. He counts quality time spent with George Benson as being amongst his most inspiring experiences to date. Ciyo has six album releases to date.

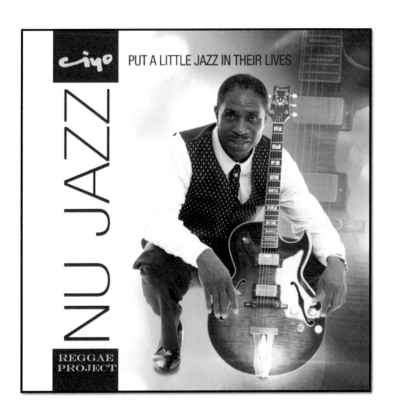

An insight into the person behind the music section

What set you on the path of music in the 1st place?
My mother and father. My father taught me to play the
guitar having come from a long line of guitarist going back
many generations in Jamaica. I then studied the classical
guitar for a couple of years as a child.

Where did you grow up; was it a musical environment?
I grew up and went to school in Birmingham. I eventually moved to London in my late teens.

What academic subjects did you study growing up? Did you plan on being a musician?
I graduated in Social Sciences with Law and Philosophy, earned a Post-Graduate in Law and also Qualified as a Fellow of Chartered Institute of Legal Executives. Music has been a major part of my life. However, I have never had aspirations of pursuing music on a full-time basis. This was largely due to advice given to me by my Father from a very early age. I therefore, chose academia over a music career and chose careers in other professional areas.

1st Guitar? How did you acquire it?
My Father bought me a Spanish guitar at the age of nine. It was a Christmas present, as my father spotted in me, from a very early age, i.e., three years of age, that I had a particular interest in guitar. I cannot remember the make of it. My father owned a Yairi Classical guitar which I also had access to. My first electric guitar was made by a company called Gherson. It was an SG copy of a Gibson SG. Both my mother and father bought this guitar for me.

If you had a choice of any guitar in the world? What would it be?
That is a very difficult questions as there are so many superbly made guitars out there. I am extremely happy

with the range of guitars that I currently own, I particular, the Fibonacci brand. If it came down to one 'type' of guitar, it would always be a Classical guitar.

Would you play it or put it on the wall?
Both…loooool

Any other response?
I would absolutely ensure that it was 'played in'.

Why did you choose this track?
I chose this particular track (Similitude) because it encapsulates the many Jazz Guitar Greats of several generations whom I have listened to over many years.

How would you like to be remembered?
As a person and musician who:

- always believed that it was possible to achieve high standards in life
- constantly raised the bar
- inspired, encouraged and edified others

Closing remark
I am currently an endorsee of the following companies:

1. Fibonacci Guitars Ltd (UK)
2. Thomas Blug - Amp1 Classic and Mercury Edition Amps and their full range of cabs (Germany)
3. Xvive - Wireless Systems (Japan)
4. John Hornby Skewes (UK)

5. Vintage Guitars (UK)
6. Vola Guitars (France)
7. BirdCord (UK)
8. Mambo Jazz Amps (UK)
9. LR Baggs (USA)

I continue my life in pursuit of excellence, constantly in search of the truth and to discover my ordained purpose on this earth…I'm getting there!

Ramirez Classical Guitar Instrument of desire Ciyo

Joe Pass (Italian/American Jazz guitarist)

Ed Cherry (USA)

Reuben Reynolds

Reuben Reynolds has developed a reputation as a highly skilled, reliable and sought-after freelance musician and tutor from Birmingham, working within a broad range of musical styles, bands and artists throughout the UK.

Through his consistent involvement in the Midlands music scene, roles as Music Director within Aston Performing

Arts Academy (APAA) and his experience working with a variety of acclaimed artists (including MiC LOWRY, Wayne Ellington, Soweto Kinch, Youngr, Donae'O, Kaleem Taylor, Black Voices, RAYE, Terri Walker, Manchester Inspirational Voices, and Lèkan Babalola), Reuben is known for his tireless enthusiasm, versatility and high standards.

After achieving a First-Class BA Honours Degree in Music Performance from Coventry University in 2012, he soon began teaching Guitar, Music Theory & Creative Music Production privately and in schools across the country, as-well-as working alongside a number of arts organisations (such as Birmingham Symphony Hall & Punch Records) to provide mentoring for the professional and musical development of young artists /musicians.

Choose one or two songs (originals/public domain material) so we cut out copyright issues (Please submit in a recognizable format)

- Monday Rain - Mike Patrick (The Piano Album)

- Anticipate - Martin Trotman (Let's Begin)

Questions to answer

- **Influences**

Jimi Hendrix, Joe Pass, Joe Satriani, Mike Stern, Carlos Santana, Derrick Hodge, Isaiah Sharkey, Chick Corea, Charlie Parker, Miles Davis, Bill Evans, Countless R&B

from the Motown era onwards, Michael Jackson, Jamiroquai, J Dilla.

• Inspirations

My fellow musicians, peers and collaborators within the U.K. music scene.
Other prolific musicians such as Chick Corea, Soweto Kinch, Snarky Puppy, Robert Glasper.
Stories and events about people & places (Fact or Fiction)
Visual Art & Sceneries.
Music from cultures/countries that I'm not accustomed to.
Songwriters.

• Albums

Top 10 Albums that come to mind (No particular order)

Live Today - Derrick Hodge
Virtuoso #1 - Joe Pass
Return of the Space Cowboy - Jamiroquai
LOVE.LIFE.LIVE - Isaiah Sharkey
Garvey's Ghost - Burning Spear
My Spanish Heart - Chick Corea
The Fantastic Vol2 - J Dilla
Off The Wall - Michael Jackson
Birth of Cool - Miles Davis

• Styles guitarists

I don't think I have a particular guitar style but rather a mix of the music I listen to and resonate with.

An insight into the person behind the music section

- **What set you on the path of music in the 1st place?**

A few of my friends at secondary school wanted to start a band and practice after school so I decided to play drums. I soon started to play-around with any instrument I could get hold of. It just so happened that the guitar was portable and quiet enough for me to play at home so I ended up spending more time playing that. The school music teacher was massively encouraging of my music studies so I'd say that she is one of the main reasons I became so motivated about studying music.

- **Where did you grow up; was it a musical environment?**

I grew up in Birmingham. Erdington, mostly. My parents played music loud & often. There'd be various types of Pop, Soul & Reggae music and so some of my early music discovering was via my parents CD/Tape rack. I didn't really come into contact with instruments until my teenage years.

- **What academic subjects did you study growing up did you plan on being a musician?**

Music, Art & Drama were the subjects I had a particular affinity for in school. After compulsory education, I went straight on to study music in college and then university so

I didn't study any academic subjects at more than a secondary school level.

- **1st Guitar? How did you acquire it?**

Yamaha APX5a. My uncle gave it to my dad to learn and I started learning on it soon after.

- **If you had a choice of any guitar in the world?**

What would it be?

Probably a Michael A Lewis - Dream Feather.

Would you play it or put it on the wall?

I'd PLAY that thing!

Any other response?

I first saw it featured in a rare-guitar calendar years ago and loved the way it looked and the fact that it was an arch-top style guitar with 7 strings.

Why did you choose this track?

Monday Rain - I particularly like the way my guitar solo was mixed here and it's a lot of fun to play with this laidback kind of rhythm and progression. I recorded it one night from my home recording set-up.

Anticipate - I like the delicate interaction between my Acoustic Guitar and the piano melodies throughout this track. This is something that Martin (the composer & producer) was keen to achieve and so he asked me for a subtle guitar part that could support the piano melodies. This was also recorded from my home set-up.

How would you like to be remembered?

I'd like to be remembered as having a positive impact on other people, whether personally or through music.

Closing remark(s)

Michael A Lewis - Dream Feather. (Reuben Reynolds
instrument of desire)

Chris Cobson

Guitarist **Chris 'Santo' Cobson** was born in Ghana and grew up in West London. His father played guitar and his uncle was a teacher of Ghanaian percussion and music.

Early exposure to music was as a young child when his father had regular visits and jam sessions with fellow Ghanaian musicians, including Osibisa founder Teddy Osei and Pete Vanderpuye who played saxophone for Johnny Nash. Chris was fortunate to attend a secondary school that had a large music department including four big bands!

His father was a Jazz guitar enthusiast and regularly played records by Wes Montgomery, Grant Green, Kenny Burrell and George Benson. These artists were to become Chris' biggest influences. His love of Jazz led him to study firstly at Goldsmiths College then the Guildhall School of Music and Drama. However, it was mainly through listening and transcribing the recordings of the great Jazz Masters where Chris received his Jazz education. Chris soon became much in demand and noted for his versatility. He also taught guitar for various education establishments. His musical journey has reflected his knowledge of many guitar styles. He has played with Osibisa, Courtney Pine, The JBs (Maceo Parker, Pee Wee Ellis, Fred Wesley), Monty Alexander, Andy Sheppard, Ronnie Scott's Big Band, Shelia Ferguson, S.E Rogie, Gasper Lewal, Dick Heckstall-Smith, Jim Mullen, David Newton, Omar, Ebony Steel Band and many other artists from all genre of music. Chris has also performed in various theatre productions including West End shows such as Grease and Soul Train. He has played all over the world including festivals in South Africa, Singapore, Japan, Zanzibar and Ghana.

Chris has also worked extensively as a solo guitarist in the corporate function scene, where he has played at many high-profile events.

More recently Chris has been the guitarist in London's Ivy Club house Jazz trio and a member of the Courtney Pine 'House of Legends' tour. He is also a prolific songwriter and arranger.

- **Influences**

My influences are all the Jazz Greats. Blues guitarists such as Blind Blake, Freddie King, B.B King, Robert Johnson. Osibisa, Fela Kuti, Ali Farka Toure, E T Mensah, Bob Marley.

- **Inspiration**

I am inspired by listening to all the above musicians, and world music.

- **Album**

The albums I recall having a big impact on me are:

Boss Guitar (Wes Montgomery), Giant Steps (John Coltrane) Bird with Strings (Charlie Parker) Kind of Blue (Miles Davis) Lady in Satin (Billie Holiday) Soul Station (Hank Mobley) Midnight Blue (Kenny Burrell) Solid (Grant Green) Love Supreme (John Coltrane)

I enjoy all guitarists and styles ranging from Paco De Lucia, Hank Marvin, Jimi Hendrix, Freddie Green.

Insight into person…

I have always loved music, but the quest to be as good as Wes Montgomery set my path to be a musician.

I studied the usual academic subjects such as English, Maths, History, French etc, and initially wanted to be a journalist.

First (proper) guitar was a Kay Strat. I paid weekly instalments of £1 to buy it.

Choice of guitar would be a vintage Gibson L5. Would definitely play it! (after staring at it on the wall for about a week).

I chose the track because it's an original which shows my musical influences and it also features the great Courtney Pine.

Would like to be remembered (but not so soon brah) as a Guitarist who could play many styles and write great songs.

Gibson L5 (Guitar of desire Chris Cobson)

Ivan Christie

Ivan Christie, also known as Natchylus the Guitarist, has largely contributed to the music industry since 1978 to date. He started to perform at age seven years old, taught by his father, who was also responsible for introducing him to Jamaican popular music via the Radiogram. Ivan has worked alongside, supported and featured on scores of bills with an impressive number of well-known UK artists such as, Sandra Cross, Sylvia Tella, Peter Hunnigale, Carroll Thompson, Janet Kay, Vincent Nap, Vivian Jones, Trevor Walters and The Investigators, to name but a few.

Ivan has also worked alongside and appeared on the bill with singers on a global scale including, the Wailers, John Holt, Mykal Rose, The Manhattans, Millie Jackson, Jean Carne, Lukie Dee, Alton Ellis, Christopher Ellis, Josey Wales, Ginger Williams, Susan Cadogan, Little Roy, Jimmy Cliff, Morgan Heritage, Max Romeo, Levi Roots, Mikey Spice, Richie Spice, Gappy Ranks, Toyin Adekale, The Fugees, Elton John, James Brown, Buju Banton, Luciano, Culture, Ken Boothe, Burning Spear and Third World, in short, the vast majority of Reggae fraternity. In fact, over the years Ivan has performed on several music entertainment platforms, some of which are showcased on the BBC and social media, he has been very instrumental in the arranging and recording of various artists and currently has his own album entitled Cool Reggae released on the 1st of May 2020.

Furthermore, Ivan is also the author of 'The History and Development of Reggae Music'. Indeed, Ivan's legacy is one not to be reckoned with, as such he is highly respected by many. His current studio was built to further support the production and promotion of Reggae and such like music.

Here is the information you required as follows:

- **Influences**

My main influences are in Ska, Rock Steady, Reggae and Dub; ranging from artist such as Skatalites, Toots And The Maytals, Bob Marley Alton Ellis, Dennis Brown, Ken Boothe, John Holt, Gregory Isaacs, King Tubby's, etc.
Also influenced by classic Soul, Blues, Jazz and Funk from 60s 70s and 80s especially Motown. But has a special affection for the classic Studio 1 and Treasure Isles era 1968- 1975, which includes some of the artist aforementioned, in particularly Alton Ellis and Ken Boothe. Also not forgetting the church where I first got my experience as a young boy.

Inspirations

My inspiration first comes from my father who put a guitar in my hands and **taught** me the first chords I ever knew.

My mother for her humility.

Bob Marley for his message.

Muhammad Ali for his self-belief and determination.

Nile Rodgers for showing the **world that rhythm guitar could lead from the front e.g., Sister Sledge I'm** Thinking Of You.

Al Anderson, lead guitarist. His lead solos inspired me to attack lead guitar more.

Not leaving out the great George Benson with all the beautiful melodies he played on his instrumental albums.

He is one of the reasons that I recorded my debut album.

I would like to also mention Eric Clapton, Blues Rock genius.

Albums

I have recorded one album which is a guitar instrumental Reggae Album entitled Cool Reggae.

I have recorded on several albums:

Good Things Come by Vincent Nap

Sandra Cross Sings

Essence by Chardel Rhoden

Born Again by Chardel Rhoden

Di Captain, by Freddie McGregor

Strictly Roots by Morgan Heritage, to name but a few.

Styles Guitarist

I like George Benson's smooth style of play

Nile Rodgers' percussive rhythm

BB King's Blues makes the guitar cry with emotion

Bob Marley and Bingi Bunny (who played for Gregory Isaacs Roots Radics band) both had great sound technique for reggae riddim guitar.

My dad set me on the path of music the day he put guitar in my hand.

I grew up in North-West London. I grew up in a musical household as all my siblings sang and played an instrument of some sort of the other.

The school I went to was very musical. I played in a school 40-piece-orchestra and performed on TV by the age of 13/14. I also played in the school Steel Band and was the rhythm guitarist for a Lovers Rock band called DECISION.

I am a self-taught musician with no professional music qualifications. However, I do have a degree in Music Instrument Technology.

I did not directly plan to be a musician, but was always involved in music from a very early age. I started performing on Stage with my band Decision from the age of 14 and have been constantly involved with live and recording music ever since.

My dad bought my first guitar

My dream guitar was always a Fender Stratocaster of which I currently own the Strat Plus version.

My other choice is a Gibson Les Paul which I have not manage to own and if I did, I would definitely play it.

I chose these tracks, because they influenced from my times I spent in Jamaica.

I would like to be remembered as a decent human being who performed and produced great music.

Music is Life.

Alton Ellis   Ken Boothe (Jamaica)

Gibson Les Paul Custom (Ivan Christie guitar of desire!)

Paul Williams

Born in Manchester UK **Paul** began playing guitar at a young age. A few months after he was born, his mother bought a guitar and as soon as Paul became big enough to play, his mother introduced him to his first notes on the guitar and his musical journey began.

Later on, inspiration came from his uncle, who regularly played guitar in the reggae bands Pressure Shocks and Junior C Reaction.

It was this musical experience that opened his young ears to the importance of rhythm and groove.

Paul sees his exposure to the Church in his teenage years and throughout his life as the turning point, as this gave him the opportunity to travel and play with gospel artists and musicians throughout the country.

After a couple of years, Paul became interested in Jazz guitar whilst mixing with his fellow guitarist from the church, he began to home study jazz guitar.

During these times, Paul enrolled at his local college to study classical guitar and light music attending two nights a week.

After School Paul's mother told him he was not allowed to pursue music as a career, the words "You must get yourself a trade, you can do music on the side" were the words spoken at a careers officer meeting.

Music became his inspiration and Paul became interested in composition, after being inspired by such artists as Andrae Crouch, Take 6, Commissioned and also jazz artists like George Benson, Earl Klugh, Paul Jackson Jr, Wes Montgomery and Larry Carlton…To name but a few,

Paul began writing and producing music of his own. On July 25th 2020 Paul released his debut album entitled Colours of Joy.

After many years of working as a full-time Electronic Engineer and playing in local function bands an array of popular music, Paul kept his dream alive and finished his first album.

An album consisting of contemporary smooth jazz sounds, likened onto some of the best in the business.

Words such as incredible rhythm and beautiful melodies along with a soulful groove have all been attached to Paul's music.

Paul has shared the stage with many more great Artists being a resident guitarist of the awarding winning Gospel Show, Gospel Central in Birmingham, he has played guitar and toured with Floacist of Floetry, and over the last few years Paul has had the opportunity to play for Bazil Meade MBE Founder of The London Community Gospel Choir, Noel Robinson, Take 6 Kim Burrell, Mervyn Warren Tyndale Thomas MBE Choir Director of the Liverpool Philharmonic Choir and reggae artist Lytie Powell to name but a few of the more known Artists.

As an artist, Paul writes music to enrich the soul and enlighten the heart, taking the listener on a musical journey, the words catchy, extremely memorable, refreshing, uplifting, smooth, and groovy have all been attached to his music.

Questions to answer

· Influences

I am influenced by lots of musicians of course: George Benson, Larry Carlton, Earl Klugh Joe Pass Wes Montgomery.

· Inspirations

George Benson is my all-time greatest inspiration for playing and creating music.

I can be disheartened with my progress as a guitarist, but when I listen to some of George Bensons music, it lifts me and I'm ready to pick up my guitar again he just makes me want to play.

I also draw inspiration from the funniest of the places like Rafa Nadal winning a grand slam makes me want to keep pushing to succeed as a musician.

· Albums

Top Albums George Benson Collection,
Donald Fagen The Nightfly
Andrae Crouch Don't Give Up and many more.
Earl Klugh Soda Fountain Shuffle

Guitar Styles

Earl Klugh for the classic style
George Benson for raw groove
Larry Carlton for the singing in his music

An insight into the person behind the music section

Paul is a full-time Medical Equipment Engineer and often drives 100's of miles to different hospitals all over the UK.

Paul sees himself as someone who has friends all over the country.

Paul moved from school to school, city to city so he has friends all over the country along with his church family.

If you were to invite Paul out you would most probably find he would turn up on his own as he wouldn't have any particular friend he would take. But he may take his daughter or wife or mother.

Paul Williams grew up in Manchester Moss Side and Old Trafford he grew up in an area where there were lots of kids and friends who he built up great relationships some of them were learning to play instruments too.

This was where he could share what he was learning and learn from then be inspired too.
Paul

· **What set you on the path of music in the 1st place?**

We have quite a few musicians in my family good ones too. I think it's in my DNA put there from God that's what I believe.

· **Where did you grow up; was it a musical environment?**

Manchester Moss Side Old Trafford

Fantastic time playing steel drums learning guitar with friends and school friends discovering things at a young age.

· What academic subjects did you study growing up did you plan on being a musician?

I studied Music, Physics, Maths, Electronics.

· 1st Guitar? How did you acquire it?

I played my mum's guitar from the ages of 10 to 13 then I got my first electric guitar a Satellite Guitar my uncle picked from a local shop.

· If you had a choice of any guitar in the world?

Or I would have to have more than one the right guitar for the right job.

What would it be?

It would have to be a guitar that I could play 'cause I would want to play it.
Gibsons
Ibanez
Fender
Taylor
Godin
Eastman

No particular order

Would you play it or put it on the wall?

Nooooo......... wayyyyy.

Any other response?

I don't have a specific guitar.
As long as it fits my fingers it sounds great and makes me want to play and never put it down that's the guitar for me.

Why did you choose this track?

It's one of the first songs I wrote and produced around 20 years ago it's a good reflection of my style and the melody I think is strong.

How would you like to be remembered?

Someone whose music takes you to another place.

A great family man. A great friend. A great farther.

Closing remark

The Guitar is a beautiful personal instrument one you can carry and play anywhere.

It's the tool I use to play and communicate music the unspoken language we all understand.
I trust the music. I trust this project will take you to another place.

Ibanez GB10

(Paul Williams Instrument of desire)

Tony Remy

    Tony Remy is one of the world's most exciting guitar players of any genre. His hard-edged rhythmically driven approach is enriched with jazz intuition and bluesy soul. His ability to adapt to any style of music sets him apart from many other guitarists and is the principal reason why

Tony's name is consistently near the top of the 'must have' list. Just ask Annie Lennox, Jack Bruce, Pee Wee Ellis, Mick Hucknall, Glenn Hughes, Craig David, etc. why they called him and the answer will always be the same - "Tony Remy delivers!"

Live on stage, his relentless invention and incredible raw energy can set the crowd on fire. The reputation he has gained within the jazz community worldwide is fast making a legend out of this North London musician.

Tony started his professional music career in 1986, although he was on the Jazz scene earlier. He recalls: "I had a band called 'Cube 60' in 1984 with Winston Clifford, Joe Bashorun and Nick Cohen. We were crazy about Miles Davis, Weather Report, Steps Ahead (a.k.a. Steps) and the Brecker Brothers, so we were writing and playing that stuff. I even had a rock band called 'Secretary Bailey'," he said with a smile.

Then, in 1985 'Cube 60' developed into 'Desperately Seeking Fusion' with Frank Tontoh (Amy Winehouse, Jack Bruce, George Michael, etc.), Joe Bashorun Robin Ashland Nick Cohen Jason Rebello (Jeff Beck, Sting, etc.) and Julian Crampton (Sunburst Band, Dexys, Incognito, etc.). "That was really my first outing as co-bandleader." he proudly remembers.

Way before he released anything under his own name, Tony was hard at work as an in-demand session player, contributing quality guitar to albums by London Jazz alumni such as Cleveland Watkiss, Jason Rebello, Steve Williamson, Philip Bent, Roger Beaujolais and Jean Toussaint. Tony Remy's reputation was growing and a certain American Jazz label had taken a particular interest in this young British rising star.

Tony released his first solo album, "BOOF" in 1993 on the American Jazz-Fusion label GRP, home to the cream of Jazz artists and THE label to go to at the time. The album received excellent reviews and established Tony Remy as one of THE names to watch. Jazz radio fell in love with the sheer variety of tracks to draw upon, whilst Tony's touring schedule really began to take him to the next level.

However, following a more autonomous path, in 1997 Tony decided to release his second album "METAMORFOLLOW-G" on his own, recently created label, Alltone Records. Tony's playing stretched out even further and allowed his ideas to draw upon many of the different guitar styles which influenced him as a youngster. Guitarists such as John Scofield, Hiram Bullock, Mike Stern, George Benson, Jimi Hendrix and BB King all contributed in shaping Tony's playing, before he began to develop his own unique style.

The roster of artists who Tony has toured and recorded with reads like a veritable 'Who's Who?' of quality musicians. From the Rock & Pop world, he's played with such names as Annie Lennox, Jack Bruce, Steve Lukather, Glenn Hughes, Simply Red, Craig David, M-People, Gary Barlow and Sarah-Jane Morris. And from the Jazz, Funk & Soul world, he's played with artists as diverse as Herbie Hancock, Pee Wee Ellis, Incognito, Jazz Crusaders, Courtney Pine, Freddie Hubbard, Ronnie Laws, Joey Negro's Sunburst Band, Don Blackman, Lonnie Liston Smith, Tom Brown, Kenny Burke, Tony Momrelle (and produced his big band album), Matt Bianco, Jason

Rebello, Lenny White, Julian Joseph, Down To The Bone, David Jean-Baptiste, Lonnie Liston Smith, Keni Burke, Brenda Russell, Cleveland Watkiss, Noel McKoy, Maysa Leak, Omar, Jean Toussaint, US3, Steps Ahead and many, many more.

Amongst the vast catalogue of artists, Tony has recorded with are legends such as Herbie Hancock for his 2005 album, 'POSSIBILITIES', supporting Annie Lennox on Paula Cole's, 'Hush, Hush, Hush'. Tony also appears on the Japanese edition of Annie Lennox's 2003 album, 'BARE', performing on a 'live' version of 'Cold'.

Jazz-vocalist and renowned actress, Marianne Jean-Baptiste (Mike Leigh's 'Secrets & Lies', U.S. Drama, 'Without A Trace' and UK phenomenon, 'Broadchurch') worked with Tony to co-write the soundtrack to Mike Leigh's 1997 movie, 'CAREER GIRLS'.

In 1998, Tony was asked to play on Simply Red's 1998 album, 'BLUE', and followed this up with several live performances for their world tour.

After being a part of the Incognito alumni on the 2005 album, 'ELEVEN', which contained co-written songs from Tony; then the 2006 album, 'BEES + THINGS + FLOWERS', he and co-founder of Incognito, Jean-Paul 'Bluey' Maunick, decided to collaborate on the 2007 album, 'FIRST PROTOCOL', and created a funky, electric guitar and keyboard-based collection of songs.

Highlighting Tony's amazing diversity yet again, he created music for an art installation in the medieval castle of Piombino in Tuscany; 'Without Borders' composition,

'Solitude' allowed his music to enhance the visual aspects in a truly magical setting.

One of Tony's most recent successes is his work as co-writer, producer and musician on eclectic vocalist, Sarah-Jane Morris' 2014 album, 'BLOODY RAIN'. Featuring amazing co-musicians such as Courtney Pine, Pee-Wee Ellis, Ian Shaw and Soweto Gospel Choir, the album has had glowing reviews and has been toured around Europe and the UK.

Tony's latest collaboration with Sarah-Jane Morris is the 2019 album of music from the canon of folk hero, John Martyn; SWEET LITTLE MYSTERY and has already received glowing reviews. The album was a true labour of love to honour John Martyn's incredible body of work and Tony played on, arranged and produced the album. Tony and Sarah-Jane recently completed a triumphant 12 date residency at the 2019 Edinburgh Festival, which resulted in being awarded the Lustrum Award by Robert McDowell.

Tony has also completed work with renowned guitarist, Bernie Marsden, for a forthcoming album of acoustic interpretations of the music of Jack Bruce.

As for the concert stage, Tony played with the legendary, Jack Bruce, as part of his Big Blues Band, performing all around the world for several years, including jamming on stage with Jack and Toto's Steve 'Luke' Lukather. When Glenn Hughes needed an axeman, he called Tony Remy and dug into the Trapeze, Deep Purple and solo catalogue to stretch Tony's chops. Iconic saxman for James Brown; Pee-Wee Ellis, always uses Tony whenever he plays live and tours Europe regularly. Jazz-Funk stalwarts, Matt Bianco, never tour without the dexterity of Tony Remy as part of both their touring and studio band. Quite simply - Tony Remy is in demand.

Tony Remy continues to do what he does best - play guitar! His touring schedule is almost non-stop, but he still bathes in the warm creativity of the studio and is currently putting the finishing touches to his self-produced forthcoming own album, 'IN THE MIDDLE OF BEFORE AND AFTER'. Featuring a stellar line-up of musicians, it will please both fans and those yet to still discover Tony Remy's dazzling talents.

Hiram Bullock (USA)

Patrick Eggle Berlin Pro Instrument of desire Tony Remy

Cameron Pierre

    Born in London, **Cameron** was raised on the Caribbean Island of Dominica. Like most of his peers, Cameron's early musical influences were Bob Marley, Burning Spear, Jimmy Cliff, and a host of artists from that era of popular Jamaican music, oh, and Stevie Wonder. At sixteen, he taught himself to play the guitar, and it was within the reggae genre that he first established himself, working with Jamaican artists including Clint Eastwood & General Saint, Barrington, Levy, Al Campbell, Wayne Marshall, Dennis Brown, Tippa Irie, Micheal Prophet et al. Then came the slow discovery of George Benson and Charlie Christian, and through them, Wes Montgomery, Miles Davis and Charlie Parker. Since then, Cameron has gone on to work with Courtney Pine, Pee Wee Ellis, Orphy Robinson, Alex Wilson, Mario Conange, Jazz Jamaica, Dennis Rollins, Omar Puente, Junior Walker, Joe Cocker, Orphy Robinson, and numerous others.

As his own musical direction veered towards jazz, he remained in demand on the Calypso, and reggae circuit. A stalwart of the British jazz scene since the 80s, he was invited by renowned British saxophonist Courtney Pine to join his band and has since become an integral part of the group both as a recording and live artist.

Alongside Courtney's band, in 1994 Cameron formed 'Creole', a multi-cultural melange of musicians from Africa, Haiti, Cuba and the Caribbean, enjoying wide critical acclaim for their performances at the Glastonbury and Womad Festivals. In 1997, Cameron released the first of his five solo albums, Friday Night, to wide critical acclaim. In 2003 he also released "The Other Side of Notting Hill", a body of work which was to help cement his reputation as a guitarist/composer par excellence. As a follow up to the acclaimed 2007 release "Pad up" his most recent release, "Radio Jumbo" his 6th studio cut, sees

Cameron teaming up with French virtuoso pianist Mario Canonge for his second release on the Destin-e Label.

"Though his approach is undeniably indebted to that of his two great heroes, Wes Montgomery and George Benson, but infused with a bounce and vitality that belongs only to him. Touring with Courtney Pine's award-winning band Cameron's guitar style has dazzled many a jazz fan, and he has received glowing reviews from all over the world for his warm, dexterous sound and his self-deprecating and engaging stage presence".

- **Influences**

My main influences as a guitar player would have to be George Benson, Wes Montgomery & Pat Martino, in no particular order; but these were the big three, who really got me thinking about or rather persuaded me; you know to want to be a jazz guitarist.

My influences are as a musician not a guitarist, I really was only interested in the music that came from the Eastern Caribbean. From places like Trinidad, Calypso, Martinique and Guadeloupe, so you had Zouk, Kadas and Beguine. Also, one of the music that really helped to shape me was the music of Haiti; they have a music called Kompa.

And to be honest with you, that is the music I listen to this day! If you came into my car right now you won't be hearing Coltrane, or Wes. You'll be hearing Haiti musicians Tambu Combo, Skasha or other bands from Martinique, Guadeloupe and Dominica.

Zouka, Calypso this was the music that had a massive impact on me, and to this day it's the music I prefer to listen too. I love Jazz and the challenges that Jazz brings, but give me my music from the Eastern Caribbean every day.

Give me my Zouk, Kompa, Kadas and others, that's me. I just thought I'd add that in there.

- **Inspirations**

I actually grew up during a period in Dominica in the 70s when you know every village had a band! Literally every village had a band. You know there was one or two bands who had left Dominica and went overseas. Guadeloupe, Martinique, France, and had done really well. So that really just inspired all the young kids to be musicians. And hmm I was no different. I was fortunate, in the sense that you know this guy came from England and he had loads of equipment, and was looking for musicians to play. I just happened to be in the right place at the right time. I couldn't play anything, we all had to learn on the spot! Infact, I actually got my break in that band, when the original bass player left to become a Christian! He didn't want to play any secular music. So, I jumped in. So yeah.

- **Albums**

In terms of albums the album that did it for me was two albums, there was a George Benson album called Living inside Your Love (Warner Bros 1978!) It wasn't the first jazz album I heard, but when I decided to investigate the jazz guitar on the insistence of a friend of mine who kept going on about George Benson. I bought an album called Living Inside Your Love. And that led me to Wes Montgomery and I bought an album called Moving Wes or Far Wes. These two albums, I was dead and gone after that. There was no return for me!! My fate was sealed.

- **Styles guitarists**

The original three I mentioned, you know obviously Scofield and Pat Metheny became really popular in the 80s and 90s so it would be hard to leave them out. But really those three because they covered everything for me. Between those three (Benson, Wes, Martino) you had the Blues. You had Bebop, you had everything in there. Literally everything so there was nowhere else I needed to go. Everything I needed was there.

An insight into the person behind the music section

What set you on the path of music in the 1st place?

My dad was a jazz fanatic! He had a huge jazz record collection, but mainly vocals you know loads of Nat King Cole. I think my dad probably had every recording Nat King Cole did. Those before he became a vocalist, and those after. Loads of Sarah Vaughan, Ella Fitzgerald and Joe Pass. My mom now, listened to all the reggae stuff! All the Trojan and Stax records. So, I would be 11, 12, 13 years of age. But what really set me on a path was the village I lived in called Soufriere in Dominica. A guy showed up one day with a truckload full of equipment and it was custom back in the Caribbean (Dominica) what usually happened, we couldn't afford to purchase instruments so you would find some rich person usually coming from the States or England and they would bring down gear and they would find musicians to play, you become a band, when you start gigging, then every gig you do you pay the owner of the equipment some money. So, this guy basically he had all his equipment that he took from another set of musicians who weren't paying him and he brought it up to my village, and no one could play. There were no musicians. There was one guy who played guitar, and we thought he could play guitar but he couldn't. But you know the saying in the land of the blind the one-eyed man is King! That guy was a king because he had a guitar but he could not play. Because of this, everyone chose this instrument. Everything going nice I'm not part of the band, the band is running, musicians doing their thing, guys learning their trade they are gigging every weekend for free but they are gigging. I got interested because all of us were in the same age group so I would go there with them I would pick up a guitar and try and learn a few chords and so on it so happened one day that the bass player became a Christian and left the band and that was it. I was roped into play this bass! It had three strings because the G string on the bass the machine head was broken, we couldn't find one on the Island. Ordering one from America well, we knew very little how to obtain one of these things. So, this guitar had the E A and D string. That's what I learned to play the bass on. I was aged 16 and three months later we travelled to Martinique to record an album. Yes, but all that time I really wanted to play the guitar. However, this is how I got into this music ting!

Where did you grow up; was it a musical environment?

In the village I lived in we had one guy who played the guitar Attenas his name was. He walked around with his Yamaha Jumbo Acoustic guitar. But I tell you what used to happen, I wanted to be a guitar player and I used to hire the guitar from him! I used to pay him 1 EC Dollar for the week. I would give him the dollar on Friday take the guitar from him and needed practice. Next week he'd come back. Or maybe somebody would have intervened and they got the guitar before me. So that one guitar would be going round. That was the environment we grew up in. But what was interesting in terms of music, were the radio stations. We had a couple of radio stations that played TOP 40 music. There was no specialist radio station, (Jazz Reggae Socca) It was just a radio station that played everything. It might be Elvis today, Beatles tomorrow, Mighty Sparrow next day or instead Michael Jackson that's how the radio station worked. So, you've heard everything.

What academic subjects did you study growing up did you plan on being a musician?

I'll let you know brother, I haven't got a Secondary School Education. I left school at the age of 14 maybe even 13. Ermm though, you know what it is like you are a young man with no guidance, you will do what you want to do. I found myself in a situation where I lived with my grandmother, my mom was in England, my dad was on the other side of the island, we didn't really have a relationship per say. My grandmother fell ill and was in hospital for 8 months. So there I was as a 13/14-year-old having to look after my gran; so, I basically didn't go back to school after that. Fortunately, music intervened.

1st Guitar? How did you acquire it?

That's a really strange story! Now I'm in Dominica and I'm playing Bass with this band. And we have just released an album I'm aged 16, 17 around 17 I would say and erm things going nice man, little celebrities in the village. I wrote to my mom and I said to my mom "can you send me a bass guitar" because the bass guitar we had only had three strings. It was this huge semi-acoustic bass with Flat-wound strings. Imagine I used to be skinny in those days and this guitar used to look huge. Imagine those old films with the Beach Boys those American Bands playing those big semi-acoustics, that's what it was. Anyway, I wrote to my mom and said I need a Bass Guitar. I didn't hear from my mom, until many months later I got a letter from the airline office from Leah telling me that my fares have been paid to travel to London. *I'm like, what, that can't happen?* I'm discovering girls. I'm a celebrity! I've got an album out. We're doing gigs chuuh, I vex. Anyway, I got a ticket to travel to London. That was it. I came up to London 17/18yr. I got here to London and about a week after I got to London I still vex, vex vex proper. I was in my room one day and the door knocked and my mom walked in and she handed me this case and I said "yes, my Bass". When I opened the thing up boy, it wasn't a bass. Yuh no. It was a plank of wood with six strings. This cheap cheap Kay catalogue guitar; because it had Raven written on the top with six strings. I just looked at the guitar and thought boy how do I tell my mom you bought the wrong guitar? Because I know she struggling already. It's she alone, she and my dad divorced. So, I couldn't tell her she bought the wrong guitar, so I just had to get on with it. So that's how I really became a guitarist; by pure accident, because I really loved the bass and wanted to carry on with the bass. That's how I got my 1st guitar.

If you had a choice of any guitar in the world?

What would it be?

Ok, I don't like owning guitars that I don't use! I find it hard to have a guitar there as an ornament under the bed. If I am not using the guitar, I will get rid of it. I remember back in the day in the 80s I used to salivate over a Mesa Boogie amp a 335 guitar, that sort of thing you know, and of course I got into the position where I could have those things and then I didn't want it. I've had the 335s I've had the Mesa Boogies I've had all of these. And for me any guitar I find if it's working and I like it, I'll keep it! But I don't really salivate over you know you must have an L4 or a L5, no I'm not like that. I mean the best guitars I've played have been surprisingly cheap. So, no, I don't do that with guitars.

Why did you choose this track?

If you listen to the track, you'll know the changes are on John Coltrane's tune called Giant Steps. You know Giant

Steps every jazz musician wants to conquer it. It's the Mount Everest of Jazz Tunes. Everybody wants to play it. I mean I could never really play that tune properly. No matter how hard I tried. But I love it It's such a simple melody, but a great melody you know. It's a challenge. We were flying back from a gig and I was sitting next to Courtney (Pine CBE) and we were talking about it. I was thinking about doing it as a Bossa Nova, he mentioned someone else as already done that. He said why don't you just put a new melody on the chords? I'm like yeah genius. So, you know same chords I just stretched the sequence a little making it one chord per bar and just changed the melody. Throw a socca beat on that and there you go.

How would you like to be remembered?

As a guitarist who was true to himself and stuck by his convictions I tried. I tried my best. When I went on stage. I left everything on the stage, I didn't hold back. So, these are the sort of things I'd like to get across.

Closing remark

We must try harder. We definitely must try harder. I believe there are few of us now in positions of influence. And I think we have to take advantage of these positions that we have obtained because you know we won't be here forever. Few of us who have achieved certain things, who are in a position of influence should really sit down and try and find a way to make those influence. To me, it's useless just having a (expletive, pardon my French) OBE or OBR or MBE you know and then it's just a bunch of letters next to your name. It doesn't mean Jack; if you can't really put it to use. And I don't mean putting it to use for your own usage, but rather the community. I hope that helps

This project is about:

UK Based Guitarists of African/Caribbean/Duel Heritage

Squire Telecaster HH (Instrument of desire) Cameron Pierre

Edison Herbert

George Benson (USA)

Edison Herbert is a sensitive and melodic musician who plays the guitar from the heart.

Encouraged by his parents from the Caribbean Island of Nevis, Edison studied classical piano at The Yorkshire College of Music. However, the journey really began when he heard one of his favourite musicians play the guitar. Immediately captivated by its sound, he started the task of teaching himself.

Later Edison was awarded a scholarship to The Guildhall School of Music and Drama where he studied Jazz. There he performed with The Guildhall Big Band featuring Randy Brecker at a series of shows at the famous Ronnie Scott's Jazz Club. After being heard at Ronnie's he was asked to join the jazz warriors.

Edison heads up a jazz trio featuring Neville Malcolm one of the finest bass players in the country and Winston Clifford, a best British Jazz Awards drummer. In 2015 Edison was sponsored by The Art's Council to record an album and perform a concert series.

He appeared in the Sky Arts series "Guitar Star". On performing an original tune George Benson commented, "You played the cr*p out of that brother. I really enjoyed your playing. You're one of the few cats who can make that thing sound so good."

Edison's time spent with George, his musical hero and mentor, inspiring, moving and educational.

Edison's latest **sensational album, 'Time For Love' is here.**

It's catchy, vibrant and engaging.

There are so many great musicians, past and present to choose from, but I'll start with early guitar influences. These would include an unknown church guitarist many years ago called Ernest James, he was one of the first guitarists I heard and every time I listened to him, he amazed me.

My main influences are George Benson, Wes Montgomery and Grant Green. Those three guys all had the gift of how to connect with their audience. They could play music for the intellectual Jazz listener but at the same time connect with everyone. I could reel off a whole list of guitarists that are amazing, but these three were and still are at the top of my list.

I also appreciate other instruments and styles. There are so many great players, Oscar Peterson, Joe Pass, Earth Wind And Fire, Quincy Jones, James Ingram, Ohio Players, Cory Henry and also some of the guys on the UK scene. I start back in the day and gradually work my way forward. As you can see, there's so much to get through before you get to musicians of today. There are some amazing young players coming up all around the world.

- **Inspirations**

For the most part, my early listening was Black American artists. All of which were outstanding. Ella Fitzgerald with Oscar Peterson, Nat King Cole, Billy Preston, George Benson, Monty Alexander etc. Everyone knows who they are.

Move in a few years when I left Leeds and relocated to London, I used to go and hear Alan Weekes, Jim Mullen,

Tony Remy among others. I always remember watching
Kenny Burrell perform at Ronnies.

Two inspirational Albums.
George Benson 'In Flight',
Wes Montgomery - Full House

Insight into the person.

Edison grew up in Leeds and is the youngest of three. He
and his brothers were encouraged to study classical piano
and he attended Yorkshire College of Music where he
passed his Grade 8 Pianoforte exam. Edison has always
been encouraged by his older brother Philip who is a
classical composer.

At an early age, Edison began teaching himself the guitar,
through books watching and listening to other musicians.
He was surrounded by musicians at his local church and
gained valuable experience playing for various groups and
singers on both the piano and guitar.

In 1984 Edison moved to London to study. Edison has a
B.Ed.(Hons) and has worked in education over the years.
He later was awarded a scholarship to attend The Guildhall
School Of Music and Drama where he studied Jazz
gaining experience in arranging and composition from his
lecturers. The highlight of the year was performing at
Ronnies with The Guildhall Big Band featuring Randy
Brecker.
Edison was the guitarist in west end musical
'Unforgettable' which then toured the UK, USA and Hong
Kong, Japan and Singapore. Edison has performed with
various musicians. He is a bandleader and has released a

Trio album featuring Neville Malcolm on Bass and Winston Clifford Best Jazz Drummer 2018 British Jazz Awards.

Edison took part in the Sky Arts series – Guitar Star, where he was fortunate enough to be mentored by his hero George Benson. George complimented his playing and continues to mentor Edison.

Edison is soon to release a new album which features band leader Edison Herbert – Guitar and keys, Neville Malcolm - Bass, Peter Adam Hall – Drums and Sean Hargreaves – Piano/ Keyboards.

Chosen Song

I have chosen 'Why Not?' from my album 'Time For Love'. It has catchy melody and has a real feelgood bounce and in these times it's great to be able to use music talent to uplift the mood of the people.

Guitar of choice.

At present the guitar of my choice is a 30-year-old Heritage H575. It has great wood and has a distinctive sound. When GB heard it the first thing he said, 'You got a good one there, It's the wood.

How I'd like to be remembered

Being a musician has many challenges. Just when you think you've got it, you realise there's still work to do. For me, I see this as my life's journey. There will always be something more to learn. Music is a wonderful form of communication with others. I would like to be remembered as someone who touched the hearts and minds of people through my music.

In closing

The guitar has brought me so much joy. Like any instrument there are many challenges and everyone has to find their own voice. Over the years, I have spent time appreciating many talented players. My hope is that we can all pass on our knowledge to each other and encourage UK audiences to embrace the wonderful array of Black talent that's waiting to be heard and appreciated.

Heritage Jazz Guitar (Instrument of desire) Edison Herbert

Ollie Pinnock

Orvil (Ollie) Pinnock

Ollie's musical journey started in the humble Black Country in the West Midlands, United Kingdom. He loved listening to his dad's radio (Dad loved Radio 4!) He would tune in/out to Radio 1 and other music stations and listen to the popular music of the time, even though they were from a Christian family, his parents were not that strict on what music he would be allowed to listen to. They had a small collection of 45s on vinyl, also LPs.

In the summer of '76, his sister came to live with them from Jamaica, and purchased a ukulele for his birthday, this was the beginning of his love for the guitar. He got his first opportunities to play at his local church, when a new pastor arrived with his family. Their son was already playing guitar at the time, he tried to glean from him the chords to help in his Sunday worship sessions.

He bought his first guitar, a L/H Tanglewood Strat copy in sunburst, though he longed for a Les Paul. He had no formal music training at school, but did invest in music videos, magazines, had lessons with individual players and spent many hours listening and trying to improve his musical knowledge/skills, then joined his first band 'Imani'.

He played at many gospel concerts, weddings, functions and for many talented local artists, which led to sessions with some known artists like:

First band Imani (1996) (Guys big-up yourself). Siani (2007) Alvin Slaughter (USA Gospel Artist) Belinda Kae, (2013) Cleo Higgins (Cleopatra 2013). A few gospel choirs. Gospel Central, (2013), reggae artist Sandra Cross, Peter Spence, Tippa Irie, (2015) 80s artist, Jackie Graham, Gwen Dickey (Rose Royce) Andy Abraham, (2014), Clem Curtis, Kirk Whalum, (2015). Midlands based gospel artist Divine (2015). Sandra Godley (2017) a few local cover bands, (2017), Chevelle Franklyn, Carlene Davis (JA Gospel Artists) (2020). Currently with Urban Soul Family, P.L.C.C. (Local Church) Martin Trotman (Smooth Jazz). Samantha Jayne (Sax). J.A. Reggae Band (Theatre Production).

He is presently the M/D and guitarist for J.A Reggae Band, a musical production called 'Rush, a joyous Jamaican journey, which highlights, through music, the achievements, contributions and life experiences of the African/Caribbean community in the United Kingdom, namely the Windrush generation. The show is a rousing success and well worth seeing.

• **Influences**

I have been influenced by the likes of Paul Jackson Jr, Frank Gambale, Jimi Hendrix, George Benson, Jonathan Butler, just to name a few. So many guitarists on music tracks I admired, some of them we have never heard of, but their contribution has been invaluable to me. I seek to be that musician, to be relevant to the track I'm playing on.

• **Inspirations**

I got my first opportunities to play at my local church, when a new pastor arrived with his family. Their son was already playing guitar at the time, I tried to glean from him the chords to help me in my Sunday worship sessions, and also got a 'no name' guitar that I could use. These times were, and still are precious to me. I learnt how important it was to listen and give space to other instruments. I developed a love for hymns. There was such a richness in the words they were portraying, always speaking of a better day/time, God's goodness/grace etc. That has continued even until the present.

• **Albums**

Collaboration, George Benson/Earl Klugh. Jonathan Butler 1987 album. Breezing George Benson. Kool and The Gang. BeBe/CeCe Winans (Heaven album).

• Styles guitarists An insight into the person behind the music section.

• **What set you on the path of music in the 1st place?**

In the summer of '76 my older sister arrived from Jamaica to live with us. This sparked the beginning of my love for the guitar, it was my birthday. It was the first time I remember being spoilt as a child. My sister and I went together to the indoor market in West Bromwich. She said I could have whatever I wanted from the 'toy-stall'. Looking around I saw a ukulele which caught my eye. She purchased it for me and I was elated, just fascinated by its sound. I spent time trying to make it sound like some of the tunes I heard on the radio, to the possible annoyance of my siblings, I discovered in all of this joy, I was holding it the 'wrong' way due the fact, I was left-handed.

- **Where did you grow up; was it a musical environment?**

My musical journey started in the humble 'Black Country in the West Midlands, United Kingdom. I loved listening to my dad's radio (he loved Radio 4!) I would tune in/out to Radio 1 and other music stations and listen to the popular music of the time, even though we were from a Christian family, my parents were not that strict on what music we were allowed to listen to. We had a small collection of 45s on vinyl, that was my dad's collection, as well as our sacred records (LPs) that we would play on a Saturday and sometimes Sunday on the radiogram.

- **What academic subjects did you study growing up did you plan on being a musician?**

I enjoyed learning, I was good at Maths and English and thought about being an accountant which wasn't to be, I loved playing music, but didn't plan to be a musician until opportunities started coming my way over time. I had no formal music training at school, but did invest in music videos, magazines, had a few lessons with individual players and spent hours listening and trying to improve my skills, then joined a band.

• 1st Guitar? How did you acquire it?

The ukulele my sister purchased for me in the summer of '76 for my birthday.

• If you had a choice of any guitar in the world?

What would it be?

If I had a choice of any guitar? Mmmmm, I love gadgetry, so something Les-Paul esc, (without the weight, but without compromising on the sustain) exotic wood for an exotic sound I suppose, noiseless pickups... I have large fingers, so jumbo frets, a fretboard that can switch when recording (say a midi fretboard, ideal for recording).

Would you play it or put it on the wall?

I would seek out opportunities to use it. A favourite guitar should be played regularly, the wall should be reserved for pictures.

Any other response?

Why did you choose this track?

The track I chose is called "Smile', taken off an EP from a band, Urban Soul Family. I co-wrote this tune with my musical partner in 'crime' Patrick White. Enjoy....

How would you like to be remembered?

Thinking long and hard, I would like to be remembered for being a genuine, hard-working God-fearing, respectable man who made a difference in the lives of others as well as in my own, through music, encouragement and work.

Closing remark(s)

I'm grateful to God for my playing opportunities. I've worked with some talented people, first band Imani (guys big-up yourself). Midlands based gospel group Divine. Alvin Slaughter (USA). Belinda Kae, a few gospel choirs. Gospel Central, reggae artists, Sandra Cross, Peter Spence, Tippa Irie, 80s artist, Jackie Graham, Gwen Dickey (Rose Royce) Andy Abraham, Cleo Higgins (Cleopatra) Kirk Whalum, a few local cover bands. Currently: Urban Soul Family, Martin Trotman (Smooth Jazz) Samantha Jayne (Sax). J.A. Reggae Band (Theatre Production) I'm still working on myself as an artist/player/man/father/Christian/humanitarian.

Gibson Les Paul Custom Silverburst (Instrument of desire)
Ollie Pinnock

Andrew Smith

I am a musician with extensive experience in the world of live music and studio performance. I'm currently on tour with "The King of Pop", the world's number one Michael Jackson tribute show, (from March 2018 to present), as well as being the guitarist for Heather Small (M People), and the musical director of the soul artist Jocelyn Brown. Throughout the last twenty years, I have worked with some of the UK's finest musicians and singers as well as some well renowned international artists. My first musical experience was gained from a gospel background. I started playing the guitar and bass from a very young age and honed my talents playing for choirs and gospel bands. Opportunities soon came my way that would propel me onto the pop scene.

Some of my most memorable highlights would be the recording of Lauryn Hill's multiplatinum selling album "The Miseducation of Lauryn Hill", world tours with "5ive", and the last five years on the road with the 55 million record selling "Westlife"; touring Europe, Asia, Australasia and Africa. Lately, I felt the need to go back to my roots so embraced working closely with The Peniel Place Music Services in providing tuition for schools and colleges, giving back to the community that so graciously gave to me over so many years.

I also work for a music company called Emusic which is based in schools and universities. I believe the wealth of experience and knowledge base I have obtained throughout my musical career gives me much to offer in the way of artistry, education, and training.

The following is a list of artists I have worked with and still continue to work with: Joss Stone, Michelle John, Tito Jackson, Kevin Hart, Lauryn Hill, Westlife, Rod Stewart, Alexandra Burke, Blue, Lemar, Gwen Stefani, 5ive, Chipmunk, Rhian Benson, Jamiroquai, Amy Winehouse,

Shakira, All Saints, George Michael, Mica Paris, Belinda Carlisle, Lulu, Eternal, Gabrielle, Take That, E17, Des'ree, Lynden David Hall, Omar, Gloria Gaynor, Deniece Williams, Nu Colours, N'Dea Davenport, Eric Benet, Beverly Knight, Brownstone, Joycelyn Brown, ABC, Vaya con Dios (Belgium), The Jones Girls, Matt Goss, Keith Sweat, Hamish Stuart, Noel Mckoy, Alisha's Attic, Shiro Sagisu, Misia, Ken Haru, Chemistry, The Osaka Gospel Choir, Carlyn, Ava Leigh, Jamelia, LCGC, Mushtaq, Mis-Teeq, Fierce, Jean Carne, Don. E, China Black, Billie Piper, Atomic Kitten, MN8, Cleopatra, Damage, Joe.

TV Appearances: Des O'Connor, Prince Charles 50th Birthday, Blue Peter, Children In Need, Top Of The Pops, CD UK, MTV Unplugged, Prince This Morning, This Morning, Songs of Praise, First Light, TFI Friday Boxed Set, Later With Jools (Holland).

I have had the opportunity to work in Japan for many years live on TV and in the studio, highlights being a 2004 tour with Japanese pop sensation Misa. This was a sold-out stadium tour on which I played guitar and provided backing vocals. Another major highlight was being asked to arrange a song for the Manga cartoon film "The End Of The Evangelion". The song was called "Thanatos" which climbed to a number two hit on the Japanese Pop Charts. I have played on so many film sound tracks for legendary Japanese film composer and producer Shiro Sagisu, it would be difficult for me to add it on to my CV. But the most recent was another Manga film trilogy called "The Bleach".

Continuing with my work in Japan, I was invited to work on a jazz project with a group of Japan's finest jazz musicians on an East meets West collaboration project. I'm also in the middle of producing two tracks for "The Shiro Sagisu Christmas Album" which will be released at Christmas in Japan 2019.

Dee Ral

DeeRal - Framus Guitars

Born in London, English/Jamaican.

Started playing guitar at the young age of 7. Grew up and went to a public school in Aveley, Essex.

First influences were rock bands such as 'Thin Lizzy' 'Van Halen' 'Led Zeppelin' and at the age of 16 formed his first rock band and went on the rocky road for the first time.

A few years later, met singer 'Paul Di'Anno' who had just left 'Iron Maiden' at the time and together formed a new rock band 'Battle Zone'

Many bands later in '97 after establishing himself also as a singer/ songwriter, DeeRal signed his first deal where he met singer Michelle Gayle. Together they wrote an album and went to LA to record with producer Harvey Mason Jr.

This led on to work with many other chart artists i.e., Louise, Eternal, Craig David, Mariah Carey, Darius, Spiller, Go West, Victoria Beckham, Mica Paris and more recently Anastacia.

Anastacia (USA)

Framus Electric Guitar (Instrument of desire) Dee Ral

Joseph Ross

My name is **Joseph Ross** and I'm a professional full-time Guitarist... for 30 years to be exact...

I actually first picked up a Guitar when I was 5. I was raised and brought up by my mother and father (now deceased) in a Godfearing home.

My father was a Pastor and my mother was a Gospel Singer... music was a huge part of our upbringing. I learned to play by ear from a young age in church experimenting on Drums and also Bass Guitar before settling on The Electric Guitar... into my teenage years I started to get a reputation as a sought after Guitarist playing for various choirs, soloists and groups... all this was preparation to be a full-time pro which I embarked on in 1990 until present day.

I've been blessed to work with artists such as James Brown, George Michael, Patti Labelle, Lionel Richie, Brenda Russell, Will Young, Girls Aloud, S Club 7, JLS, Eternal, BeBe Winans and the list goes on.

From live tours to TV-specials I've also been Musical Director for JLS, Girls Aloud, Sugababes, S Club and Will Young.

I've also appeared on various TV shows such as Top of the Pops, Graham Norton Show, Jonathan Ross Show, Parkinson, Jools Holland, Strictly Come Dancing, and The X Factor.

It has been a triumph doing what I do but not without its trials either, the aim is to record my own music while still being able to tour with some of the World's biggest artists.

I've recorded with various artists on albums and singles like Brenda Russell, Will Young and Fleur East...

https://open.spotify.com/track/1MxU9V13oaO148ZJYA EQXW?si=WAsW0ItaRoqG6SQLkGBpNQ

https://open.spotify.com/track/6b3dW8v4tomgyRLilNH
Gjr?si=nTM-7BacRcactUY0KIjAHQ

My influences are Gospel, Funk, Blues and Soul. My biggest inspiration was the late Trevor Prince, a phenomenal person, Guitarist and Mentor to myself and others. Albums by the likes of Chic, Earth Wind and Fire, George Benson, Andrae Crouch and The Winans really whet my musical ear and also style of guitar playing with Nile Rodgers and George Benson being big influences along with Paul Jackson Jr., Gary Moore and Steve Lukather.

I wasn't great at school sadly and was expelled at 13 and as a result have no qualifications. But music was what I enjoyed most at school.

I love Fender and Gibson Guitars... my first Guitar was a Strat which I bought on HP when I was 17yrs old... my dream Guitar would be a Gibson 335 which I would happily play for pretty much anything I would do.

I'd hope my legacy would be I took risks and made it to the stage with some of the World's biggest artists without any education but by sheer will, hard work and of course God's undeniable favour... oh, and also, I was a pretty decent Guitarist with my own style.

Gibson 335 My instrument of choice – Joseph Ross

Ian Lewinson

Ian Lewinson is a London based guitar player and band leader who has recorded or performed with a range of artists. These include Annie Lennox, Amy Winehouse, Des'ree, Emma Bunton, Paulette Tajah, Kofi, Micky Graham, Amy Studt, Kate Deraugo, Jessy Dixon, Mindgap, Shelley Twinn and Michael Mendez. He has performed in Europe, America and throughout the UK and has also played at festivals, functions and in musical theatre.

Growing up in Coventry, Ian was surrounded by talented musical siblings namely Pete and Steve Lewinson and together they worked with inspiration from their parents Ileen who played the piano and Rev Issachar Lewinson who played the guitar. Ileen would spend hours supporting her children to hone their musical talents and she encouraged her children to experiment with different musical ideas.

Ian's early musical experiences were rooted in gospel music and this environment enabled him to develop a good ear and to gain experience of blending different styles of music.

At the age of 19 Ian moved to London to take a bachelor's degree in Social Sciences and eventually went on to complete an MA in Educational Management. Shortly after coming to London Ian discovered the music of Wes Montgomery, George Benson and Grant Green who became major sources of inspiration. He developed a passion for jazz inspired guitar and regularly went to watch London based guitarists such as Alan Weeks, Cedric West, Tony Remy and Jim Mullen.

At the age of 24 Ian went to America to play at an event with his Westone guitar. Whilst in America he saw a Gibson 347 and was able to part exchange his Westone following a loan from his father. This became his main guitar and his pride and joy.

Ian did not become a full-time musician but instead played music around his work which included being an advice worker, counsellor, senior lecturer in care and counselling and running a training company and a Saturday supplementary school.

In 2019 Ian released his first single Mozart PC 21 with the support of his friend and accomplished bass player and producer Derek Taylor. This was a blend of jazz, reggae and classical music inspired by Mozart's Piano Concerto 21.

The instrumental featured this project is called Bounce Back and recognises the hope that we will be able to move forward from the cloud of 2020. It features Ian's son WesLi D, Calvin Robb, Dwayne Burke and Derek Taylor who all contributed to this project.

Ian is appreciative of the work that Derrick is doing to highlight the diversity of guitar players from the UK who are contributing, in their own way to the world of music.

Gibson ES 347 Instrument of desire (Ian Lewinson)

Tony Bean

Tony Bean was born in Handsworth, Birmingham to Jamaican Parents Eduardo and Lucille Bean.

Tony's early introduction to music came from his mother, an accomplished musician who read music, and played